KS2
SPELLING
SATs SUCCESS
WORKBOOK

Ages 7–9

KS2
SPELLING
SATs
WORKBOOK

JON GOULDING

About this book

Spelling

Learning to spell is an important stage in your child's education. It helps to develop key life skills, especially in reading, writing and languages.

This book is designed to help your child spell increasingly difficult words accurately, confidently and consistently. It will also aid preparation for the Key Stage 2 **English Grammar, Punctuation and Spelling** test.

Features of the book

- *Key to spelling* – explains each spelling concept with clear examples.

- *Practice activities* – a variety of tasks and questions to challenge your child.

- *Test your spelling* – enables your child to check their spelling of a particular group of words.

- *Test practice* – offers practice for the spelling task in the Key Stage 2 SATs.

- *Answers* are in a pull-out booklet at the centre of the book.

Spelling tips

- Ask your child to write a sentence which includes a particular word.

- Create flash cards – write problematic words on cards and display them as a visual reminder. Read words from the cards and ask your child to spell them.

- Make spelling fun – look for words on signs, etc., and encourage word play (e.g. how many words can you make from the word *supermarket*?).

ACKNOWLEDGEMENTS

The author and publisher are grateful to the copyright holders for permission to use quoted materials and images.

Cover, P01 ©Igorrita; P04 ©Charles Whitefield, ©Andre Adams; P05 ©Nip; P06 ©Michael D Brown; P08 ©reydesign, ©sababa66; P09 ©Alexandra Petruk; P12 ©lineartestpilot; P14 ©Magenta10; P16 ©Andre Adams, ©Ron Leishman; P18 ©Miguel Angel Salinas Salinas, ©jessicafiorini, ©Yayayoyo, ©Sujono sujono; P19 ©Dawn Hudson, ©lineartestpilot, ©SNEHIT, ©insima, ©connynka; P26 ©Crisan Rosu; P30 ©Lorelyn Medina; P36 ©hkannn; P39 ©Adrian Niederhaeuser; P44 ©Rozhkovs; P46 ©Matthew Cole; P50 ©dedMazay; P54 ©Ron Leishman; P57 vlastas; P58 Teguh Mujiono, ©Memo Angeles, ©lineartestpilot, ©Cory Thoman, ©jara3000; P62 ©Matthew Cole; P64 ©SlipFloat, ©RAStudio; P66 ©Fejas; P68 ©Stephanie Lirette; P71 ©erwin cartoon; P73 ©jara3000, ©November_Seventeen; P74 ©Matthew Cole; P76 ©TheBlackRhino; P77 ©lineartestpilot; P80 ©jara3000, ©onime; P84 ©diez artwork.

The above images have been used under license from Shutterstock.com

P14 ©iStockphoto/Thinkstock; P28 ©Hemera/Thinkstock; P32 ©Clipart.com; P72 ©Clipart.com

All other images are ©Jupiterimages or © Letts Educational, an imprint of HarperCollins Publishers Ltd

Every effort has been made to trace copyright holders and obtain their permission for the use of copyright material. The author and publisher will gladly receive information enabling them to rectify any error or omission in subsequent editions. All facts are correct at time of going to press.

Published by Letts Educational
An imprint of HarperCollins Publishers Ltd
1 London Bridge Street
London SE1 9GF

ISBN 9780008294199

First published 2013

This edition published 2018

10 9 8 7 6 5 4 3 2

Text and Design ©Letts Educational, an imprint of HarperCollins Publishers Ltd

British Library Cataloguing in Publication Data. A CIP record of this book is available from the British Library.

Commissioning Editor: Tammy Poggo
Author: Jon Goulding
Contributor: Louis Fidge
Project Manager: Richard Toms
Project Editor: Bruce Nicholson
Cover Design: Sarah Duxbury
Inside Concept Design: Ian Wrigley
Layout: Jouve India Private Limited
Production: Natalia Rebow
Printed and bound by Martins the Printers, Berwick-upon-Tweed

Contents

Phonically regular words

Key to spelling

Words are made up of sounds called **phonemes**. A phoneme may be made of one or more letters. Many words are phonically regular. You can 'sound out' each phoneme in phonically regular words.

cat

c-a-t

The three letters are three phonemes and spell out the word.

bread

b-r-ea-d

The five letters give four sounds (phonemes).

Recognising which phonemes have been used in phonically regular words can help you to spell them.

Practice activities

1. Write the missing phoneme(s) for each picture.

b__n

le__

__ap

h__n__

ma__k

__w__g

p__a__

c__a__

Phonically regular words

2. Look at the picture and write the correct phoneme to spell each word.

b_____t

p_____se

m_____n

m_____se

l_____t

t_____ch

p_____nt

b_____d

3. Some phonemes are represented by two consonants next to each other. Look at the picture and write the correct phoneme to spell each word.

_____ed

mo_____

ri_____

_____ips

fi_____

_____irty **30**

Test your spelling

Look at the words.

Say them aloud.

Cover the words.

Write them from memory.

Check your spelling.

ship	thing	cash
chop	ring	coat
paint	much	
this	that	

Phonically irregular words

Key to spelling

Lots of words are phonically irregular – the whole word cannot be sounded out using the individual letter sound.

people

sounds a bit like

p-ee-p-ul

table

sounds a bit like

t-ay-bul

Words such as these just have to be learned. Of course, some of the sounds you hear when you say the word aloud will help with spelling part of the word.

Practice activities

1. The words below have been misspelt. Match them to the correct spelling and practise writing the correct word. The first one has been started for you.

   a) sed   people   _____

   b) beecuz   would   _____

   c) peepul   said   _____

   d) wud   mother   _____

   e) muther   because   _____

   f) litul   sandwich   _____

   g) sanwij   little   _____

Phonically irregular words

2. Insert the correct word from the list into each sentence.

floor	shoes	pretty	climb
kind	laugh	hour	

a) I have got new _____.

b) We tried to _____ the mountain.

c) The bride wore a very _____ wedding dress.

d) He was _____ to share.

e) The train arrives in one _____.

f) The plate smashed as it hit the _____.

g) The joke made us all _____.

3. Decide whether to use **could**, **should** or **would** in each sentence.

a) It _____ rain if that cloud comes this way.

b) You _____ look both ways before crossing the road.

c) It _____ be dangerous by the river.

d) I _____ like ice-cream please.

e) _____ you mind if I went too?

f) _____ we be here?

g) There _____ be trouble ahead.

Test your spelling

Look at the words.

Say them aloud.

Cover the words.

Write them from memory.

Check your spelling.

sure	autumn	listen
thumb	great	every
could	should	
would	because	

Long and short vowel sounds

Key to spelling

The phonemes in some words are spelt the same, but have different sounds.

She is r**ea**ding a book.

This **ea** has a **long** vowel sound.

He bumped his h**ea**d.

This **ea** has a **short** vowel sound.

Sometimes a long vowel sound is split. The two vowels making the sound are separated by a consonant. The final vowel is an **e**. Adding an **e** to the word **mad** creates a split long vowel sound made by the **a** and the **e** – **made** (a_e makes the *ay* or *ai* sound).

Practice activities

1. Make some **ea** words with a **long** vowel sound. One has been done for you.

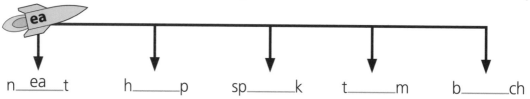

n__ea__t   h_____p   sp_____k   t_____m   b_____ch

2. Write some **ea** words with a **short** vowel sound. One has been done for you.

r__ea__d   d_____f   sw_____t   w_____ther   m_____dow

3. Make some **oo** words with a **long** vowel sound. One has been done for you.

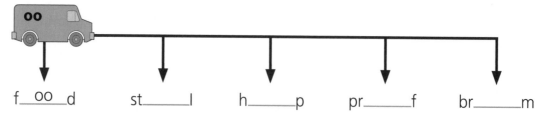

f__oo__d   st_____l   h_____p   pr_____f   br_____m

4. Write some **oo** words with a **short** vowel sound. One has been done for you.

g__oo__d   b_____k   f_____t   st_____d   sh_____k

Long and short vowel sounds

5. Insert letters to give these words a long vowel sound. Each word should fit into a sentence below. One has been done for you. Write the completed word in the correct sentence.

sh_i_n_e_   r__p__   f__n__   h__d__   c__d__   c__p__

m__d__   h__t__   p__p__   r__d__   w__n__   c__b__

a) A dice is usually a _____ shape.

b) He _____ the horse along the lane.

c) The fruit was all _____.

d) The spy cracked the secret _____.

e) Water leaked from the _____.

f) Grapes are used to make _____.

g) Most of my class _____ cabbage.

h) The weather was _____.

i) The superhero had a long, flowing _____.

j) The glass was polished to a brilliant _____.

k) Everyone tried to _____ behind the wall.

l) They _____ a den in the garden.

Test your spelling

Look at the words.

Say them aloud.

Cover the words.

Write them from memory.

Check your spelling.

beach	head	cool
hood	deaf	team
late	rode	
road	cube	

Making words plural

Singular means there is just **one** thing. Plural means there is **more than one**. Most nouns have a singular and plural form.

one dog

two dog**s**

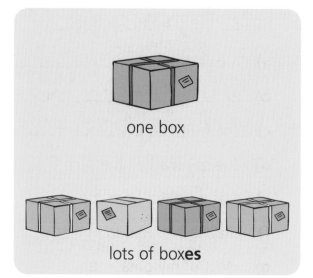

one box

lots of box**es**

You add **s** to most nouns to make them plural. However, you add **es** to most nouns ending in **ch**, **sh**, **x** or **s**.

Practice activities

1. Write the plural form of each noun. The first one has been done for you.

singular	plural
dish	dishes
kiss	
cat	
coach	
fox	
song	

singular	plural
boss	
tree	
six	
catch	
bus	
miss	

Making words plural

2. Complete these phrases with the correct singular or plural form of the noun.

   a) one dress, three _____

   b) one bush, two _____

   c) one _____, seven horses

   d) one bench, two _____

   e) one _____, three carpets

   f) one window, five _____

   g) one _____, three buses

   h) one _____, four pizzas

3. Complete the table with nouns from question 1 ending in the given letters. One has been done for you.

singular nouns ending with:			
s	x	ch	sh
			dish

Test your spelling

Look at the words.

Say them aloud.

Cover the words.

Write them from memory.

Check your spelling.

ditches	punches	patches
washes	splashes	bushes
glasses	misses	
foxes	sixes	

Syllables

Key to spelling

When you say a word **slowly**, you can hear how many **syllables** (or beats) it has. You can tap out the syllables of a word, as you say it, to help you. Breaking a word into its syllables can help you to spell it.

car

This has **one** syllable.

car - pet

This has **two** syllables.

car - pen - ter

This has **three** syllables.

Practice activities

1. Say each word slowly. Copy it and write the number of syllables.

modern	_____	_	invade	_____	_
cabin	_____	_	king	_____	_
determine	_____	_	sport	_____	_
together	_____	_	introduce	_____	_
industry	_____	_	seat	_____	_
expensive	_____	_	September	_____	_
travel	_____	_	habit	_____	_
method	_____	_	direct	_____	_
farm	_____	_	bird	_____	_

2. Write the days of the week that contain:

a) two syllables

_____   _____   _____

_____   _____

b) three syllables   _____   _____

3. Write the months of the year that contain:

a) only one syllable

_____   _____   _____

b) two syllables

_____   _____   _____

c) three syllables

_____   _____

_____   _____

d) four syllables

_____   _____

4. How many syllables are there in each word?

century   _____   **decade**   _____

millennium   _____   **year**   _____

Test your spelling

Look at the words.

Say them aloud.

Cover the words.

Write them from memory.

Check your spelling.

January	February	March
April	May	June
July	August	September
October	November	December

Compound words

Key to spelling

A compound word is a word that is made up of two smaller words joined together.

hand

+

bag

=

handbag

Each part of a compound word is a proper word on its own.

Practice activities

1. Make the compound words. One has been done for you.

   a) Add these words to **foot**: step, path, ball

   footstep _____ _____ _____

   b) Add these words to **snow**: man, storm, flake

   _____ _____ _____

   c) Add these words to **sun**: light, shine, shade

   _____ _____ _____

   d) Add these words to **rain**: bow, fall, coat

   _____ _____ _____

   e) Add these words to **hand**: bag, made, kerchief

   _____ _____ _____

   f) Add these words to **play**: ground, time, house

   _____ _____ _____

Compound words

2. Break each of these compound words into two smaller words. The first one has been done for you.

a) butterfly   butter   fly

b) newspaper   _____   _____

c) treehouse   _____   _____

d) bombshell   _____   _____

e) cupboard   _____   _____

f) doorstep   _____   _____

g) waterfall   _____   _____

h) gooseberry   _____   _____

i) waistcoat   _____   _____

3. Join words together to make compound words. The first one has been done for you.

a) bath   cake   _____

b) pan   room   bathroom

c) sauce   cup   _____

d) tooth   pan   _____

e) butter   stalk   _____

f) bean   brush   _____

Test your spelling

Look at the words.

Say them aloud.

Cover the words.

Write them from memory.

Check your spelling.

afternoon   birthday   breakfast

cloakroom   cupboard   eyesight

footstep   midnight

motorway   overcome

Different spelling, same sound

Key to spelling

Take care! Many words contain the same or similar sounds, but have different spelling patterns.

> a n**ur**se in a sk**ir**t with a lant**er**n
>
> In this example, the **ur**, **ir** and **er** sounds can easily be confused.

Practice activities

1. Underline the **er**, **ir** or **ur** sound when you copy each of these words. The first one has been done for you.

    stir   _____st<u>ir</u>_____   term   _____

    nurse   _____   church   _____

2. Underline the **ai**, **eigh** or **ay** sound when you copy each of these words.

    play   _____   eight   _____

    weigh   _____   sail   _____

3. Underline the **oi** or **oy** sound when you copy each of these words.

    boiled   _____   soil   _____

    loyal   _____   enjoy   _____

Different spelling, same sound

4. Decide whether to use **there** or **their** in each sentence.

   a) It was _____ house.

   b) _____ is always sunshine on holiday.

   c) She was always _____ waiting for him.

   d) They could not believe _____ luck.

5. Decide whether to use **hear** or **here** in each sentence.

   a) All they could _____ was the wind.

   b) It is always raining _____.

   c) What is there in _____?

   d) They did not _____ the knock on the door.

6. Decide whether to use **to**, **too** or **two** in each sentence.

   a) We would like to come _____.

   b) I am going _____ the park.

   c) There are only _____ minutes until playtime.

   d) Is it _____ late _____ buy a ticket?

   e) "It's _____ expensive _____ buy," said Mum.

Test your spelling

Look at the words.

Say them aloud.

Cover the words.

Write them from memory.

Check your spelling.

bear	bare	their
there	night	knight
here	hear	
blew	blue	

17

Words with ge and dge

Key to spelling

Apart from at the beginning of words, as in **j**am or **j**ump, **j** is rarely used to make the **j** sound. When it immediately follows a short vowel sound, it is spelt **dge**. If it follows a long vowel sound, or a consonant, the **j** sound is spelt **ge**.

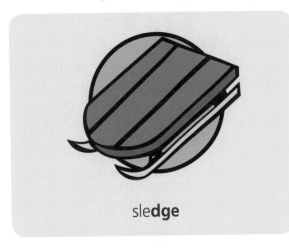

sle**dge**

hu**ge**

Practice activities

1. Complete these **dge** words.

    he_____   le_____   tru_____   bu_____

2. Complete these **ge** words.

    oran_____   hu_____   a_____   bul_____

3. Identify the **ge** and **dge** words below, underlining the letters that make the **j** sound.

garage	gadget	badge	kitchen
hedgehog	fudge	latch	wage

18

Words with ge and dge

4. Look at each picture and complete the **dge** or **ge** word.

br_____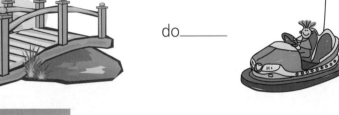

do_____

vi_____

ba_____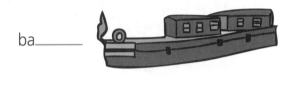

or_____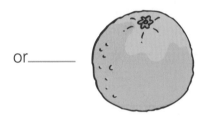

lo_____

ba_____

he_____

Test your spelling

Look at the words.

Say them aloud.

Cover the words.

Write them from memory.

Check your spelling.

badge	ledge	bridge
dodge	age	huge
orange	charge	
bulge	village	

Common word endings

Key to spelling

Look for common letter strings at the end of words. Use them to help you spell other words.

a br**ight** l**ight** at n**ight**

Practice activities

1. Make some words with common endings.

    a) –ight   r_____   f_____   t_____

    b) –ire   t_____   w_____   f_____

    c) –age   p_____   r_____   c_____

    d) –ear   cl_____   h_____   d_____

    e) –tch   fe_____   ske_____   di_____

2. Write three sentences, each containing at least two words with the same ending.

    _____

    _____

    _____

3. Make some new words, with the same ending.

   a) Change the **l** in **l**edge to **w, h, sl**.

   _____   _____   _____

   b) Change the **d** in **d**itch to **h, p, w**.

   _____   _____   _____

   c) Change the **c** in **c**are to **d, r, sh**.

   _____   _____   _____

   d) Change the **m** in **m**ore to **c, b, t**.

   _____   _____   _____

   e) Change the **d** in **d**ue to **bl, gl, cl**.

   _____   _____   _____

   f) Change the **l** in **l**ie to **p, d, t**.

   _____   _____   _____

   g) Change the **t** in **t**oe to **f, d, r**.

   _____   _____   _____

   h) Change the **t** in **t**ire to **d, s, h**.

   _____   _____   _____

Test your spelling

Look at the words.

Say them aloud.

Cover the words.

Write them from memory.

Check your spelling.

might	fright	page
enrage	dear	appear
fetch	sketch	
witch	pitch	

Adding –er, –ed and –ing

Key to spelling

When a word has more than one syllable and ends in a consonant, you **sometimes** need to double the consonant before adding the **suffix**. A suffix is a group of letters that can be added to the end of some words to change their meanings.

begin – begi**nn**er occur – occu**rr**ed Here, the **last** syllable in the root word is stressed – a greater emphasis is placed on the **last** syllable when saying the word: beg**IN** oc**CUR** So, the consonant is **doubled**.	visit – visi**t**ing limit – limi**t**ed Here, the **first** syllable in the root word is stressed – a greater emphasis is placed on the **first** syllable when saying the word: **VIS**it **LIM**it So, the consonant is **not doubled**.

If a word ends in **w**, **x** or **y** the consonant is not doubled, e.g. rela**x** – rela**x**ed, rela**x**ing.

Practice activities

1. Circle the words that **–er**, **–ed** and **–ing** can be added to.

    Say the words to check that they make sense.

    jump   cat   garden

    call   camp   stairs

2. Write out these words in the past tense by adding **–ed**. Decide whether you need to double the consonant.

    prefer _____   visit _____

    exclaim _____   hover _____

    occur _____   beg _____

Adding –er, –ed and –ing

3. Correct the sentence by changing the underlined word to its correct form.

Look out for exceptions and words which require changing in a different way.

a) When I was in Year 1, I always <u>prefer</u> to have a hot school dinner.

_____

b) Two years ago, the same argument always <u>occur</u> at the bus stop.

_____

c) The children <u>beg</u> for every penny they raised.

_____

d) There is a <u>limit</u> range of goods for sale.

_____

e) The teenagers had trouble <u>admit</u> they were wrong.

_____

f) Sunbathing is <u>relax</u>, but not if it is too hot.

_____

g) All of our class enjoy <u>garden</u> in the school allotment.

_____

h) Tomorrow I will <u>beginning</u> my homework project.

_____

Test your spelling

Look at the words.

Say them aloud.

Cover the words.

Write them from memory.

Check your spelling.

forgetting	occurred	limiting
relaxed	preferred	limited
beginning	gardening	
beginner	gardener	

23

The suffix –ation

Key to spelling

Many verbs can be changed into nouns by adding the suffix **–ation**.

inform – inform**ation**

educate – educ**ation**

Notice that when the root word ends in **e**, the **e** is dropped before adding **–ation**.

Practice activities

1. Match the correct **–ation** word to each definition.

    Use a dictionary if you are unsure about the meaning of any of the words.

admiration	imagination	aviation
evaporation	preparation	jubilation

    a) The name given to the act of preparing something. _____

    b) All about aircraft. _____

    c) Your own amazing ideas. _____

    d) Looking up to someone. _____

    e) When water turns to water vapour. _____

    f) Showing great joy. _____

2. Add **–ation** to each of the words below.

    *Remember to drop the **e** when necessary.*

    suffocate _____   innovate _____

    exploit _____   adore _____

    tempt _____   dominate _____

3. Write the verb from which each of these nouns came.

*Remember to add the **e** when necessary. Use a dictionary to help you check your spelling and the meaning of words.*

creation _____ imagination _____

education _____ information _____

preparation _____ affirmation _____

4. Complete the sentences by underlining the correct word in bold.

a) They are so good they will **dominate/domination** for years.

b) He handed over all of the **inform/information**.

c) Hot sun caused the puddles to **evaporate/evaporation** rapidly.

d) She did not want to **associate/association** with those people.

e) We sent a message to **inform/information** them how long we would be.

f) I can **imagine/imagination** a beautiful summer day.

g) Listening at school is important for our **educate/education**.

h) The pest control man came to **exterminate/extermination** the wasps.

i) They used a train to **transport/transportation** the goods.

j) Good **prepare/preparation** takes time.

k) When writing a story, use your **imagine/imagination**.

l) The artwork was all her own **create/creation**.

Test your spelling

Look at the words.

Say them aloud.

Cover the words.

Write them from memory.

Check your spelling.

information	adoration	sensation
creation	innovation	aviation
preparation	admiration	
evaporation	imagination	

The suffix –ly

Key to spelling

Look what happens when you add **ly** to some adjectives to make them into adverbs:

quiet + **ly** = quiet**ly**
gentle + **ly** = gent**ly**

happy + **ly** = happi**ly**
basic + **ally** = basic**ally**

Rule 1	Rule 2	Rule 3	Rule 4
Sometimes there is **no change** to the spelling of the **root** word.	If the adjective **ends** with **le**, you **drop** the **le** and **add ly**.	If the adjective **ends** with a **consonant + y**, you **change** the **y** to **i** before adding **ly**.	If the adjective **ends** in **ic**, instead of adding **ly** you add **ally**.

There are some exceptions to the rules:

public – publi**cly**   true – tru**ly**   due – du**ly**   whole – who**lly**

Practice activities

1. Use **Rule 1** and **Rule 4** to help you make some adverbs.

    sudden _____   basic   _____

    quick   _____   economic _____

    slow   _____   frantic   _____

    loud   _____   dramatic _____

    loving _____   athletic _____

    hopeful _____   logic   _____

2. Take the suffix off each adverb. Write the adjectives you are left with.

gladly	_____	cheaply	_____
nicely	_____	willingly	_____
proudly	_____	angelically	_____
slowly	_____	quickly	_____
comically	_____	sadly	_____
basically	_____	smartly	_____
madly	_____	stupidly	_____

3. Use **Rule 2** and **Rule 3** to help you turn adjectives into adverbs and adverbs into adjectives.

horrible	_____	possible	_____
noisily	_____	wearily	_____
heavily	_____	humble	_____
feeble	_____	idle	_____
terrible	_____	luckily	_____
angrily	_____	clumsily	_____
gentle	_____	comfortable	_____
lazily	_____	merrily	_____

Test your spelling

Look at the words.

Say them aloud.

Cover the words.

Write them from memory.

Check your spelling.

completely	usually	sadly
happily	angrily	gently
simply	basically	
frantically	dramatically	

The endings –sure and –ture

Key to spelling

Words that end in the same sound you hear at the end of trea**sure** are often spelt **–sure**, e.g. plea**sure**, mea**sure**.

Words that end in the same sound you hear at the end of pic**ture** are often spelt **–ture**, e.g. crea**ture**, na**ture**.

Be careful – the word you are trying to spell might rhyme with picture, creature, nature, etc., but it could be a root word ending in **–ch** or **–tch** with an **–er** ending, e.g. richer, catcher.

Practice activities

1. Complete each word below by writing the full word in the table.

mea	depar	plea	adven	furni
enclo	crea	lei	struc	trea

–sure words	–ture words

2. Read the words aloud and then circle those that do not use the **–sure** or **–ture** ending.

fixture	teacher	feature	enclosure	stretcher
adventure	pitcher	measure	richer	picture

The endings –sure and –ture

3. Complete each sentence with one of the words below.

A word can be used more than once.

> **measure** **treasure** **pleasure** **creature** **departure**
>
> **enclosure** **picture** **adventure** **furniture** **mixture**

a) The syrup and fruit made a sticky _____.

b) As they set sail from the jetty, their great _____ started.

c) Grandma told them off for putting their feet on the _____.

d) You should _____ your feet carefully before buying a new pair of shoes.

e) The strange _____ had blue ears, seven legs and a pink tail.

f) He always gave a friendly smile to show his _____ at meeting them.

g) The guard blew his whistle to signal that it was time for _____.

h) All of the animals were treated well and lived in a large _____.

i) Each _____ was painted with great skill and care.

j) She would always _____ the special gift he brought back from India.

k) They searched everywhere, but the buried _____ could not be found.

l) His mother said his success was a _____ of his greatness.

Test your spelling

Look at the words.

Say them aloud.

Cover the words.

Write them from memory.

Check your spelling.

measure	treasure	pleasure
enclosure	picture	adventure
creature	furniture	
departure	mixture	

The suffix –ous

Words that end in the same sound you hear at the end of danger**ous** are often spelt with the suffix **–ous**.

poison**ous**

poison (noun) + **ous** (suffix)

Sometimes the **spelling** of the **root word** remains **unchanged**.

nerv**ous**

nerve (noun) + **ous** (suffix)

Sometimes the spelling of the **root word changes** slightly. Here, the **e** has been dropped.

When the noun ends in a **consonant + y**, the **y** is changed to **i** before adding **–ous**.

If the root word ends in **–ge**, the **e** is not dropped, e.g. courag**e**ous, outrag**e**ous. Occasionally the **ee** sound, as in ser**i**ous and prev**i**ous, is spelt with an **e** as in hid**e**ous.

Practice activities

1. Add **–ous** to each of the words below.

    mountain _____   **advantage** _____

    nerve _____   **danger** _____

    fame _____   **peril** _____

2. Add **–ous** to each of these nouns. The first one has been done for you.

    fury + ous   = ____furious____   glory + ous = _____

    mystery + ous = _____   envy + ous   = _____

    victory + ous = _____   luxury + ous = _____

3. Look at these sets of suffix sums. Think about the way in which the spelling of the root word changes when **–ous** is added. Write a rule for each set to say what you have discovered.

Set A

fame + ous   = famous

adventure + ous = adventurous

_____

Set B

humour + ous = humorous

vigour + ous   = vigorous

_____

Set C

fable + ous   = fabulous

miracle + ous = miraculous

_____

Set D

mischief + ous = mischievous

_____

Test your spelling

Look at the words.

Say them aloud.

Cover the words.

Write them from memory.

Check your spelling.

poisonous	dangerous	obvious
enormous	glamorous	furious
vigorous	mountainous	
famous	tremendous	

Endings which sound like *shun*

Key to spelling

The endings **–ion** and **–ian** often have **t**, **c**, **ss** or **s** before them and the whole ending is added to the root word.

educate + **tion** = education

–tion is the ending when the root word ends in **t** or **te**. Notice that the **e** is dropped from the root word.

music + **cian** = musician

–cian is the ending when the root word ends in **c** or **cs**.

–ssion is used if the root word ends in **ss** (expre**ss** – expre**ssion**) or **mit** (per**mit** – permi**ssion**).

–sion is used if the root word ends in **d** or **se** (exten**d** – exten**sion**, ten**se** – ten**sion**), but be careful of exceptions such as atten**d** – atten**tion**.

Practice activities

1. Write out these words using the correct *shun* ending.

   invent   _____   tense   _____

   magic   _____   extend   _____

   act   _____   complete _____

   electric _____   expand   _____

2. Look at the addition of **–ssion** below.

   permit + **ssion** = permi**ssion**   transmit + **ssion** = transmi**ssion**

   What do you notice happening when **–ssion** is added?

   _____

Endings which sound like *shun*

3. Look at the list of words below.

> invention   musician   exception   mathematician   politician

Write the word that means:

a) somebody who plays an instrument   _____

b) a Member of Parliament   _____

c) when something does not follow a rule   _____

d) a newly thought of thing   _____

e) somebody who is good with numbers   _____

4. Correct the sentences by changing the underlined words to their correct form.

a) The new <u>extend</u> was nearing <u>complete</u>.

_____

b) The class had a <u>discuss</u> about using <u>express</u>.

_____

c) <u>Permit</u> was given for <u>admit</u> of infants to the disco.

_____

d) She had an <u>inject</u> to release the painful <u>tense</u>.

_____

Test your spelling

Look at the words.

Say them aloud.

Cover the words.

Write them from memory.

Check your spelling.

inflation	injection	completion
discussion	permission	extension
tension	electrician	
magician	action	

Endings which sound like *zhun*

Key to spelling

Often if a verb ends in **se** or **de**, changing the ending to **–sion** results in the **zhun** sound.

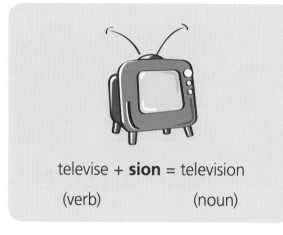

televise + **sion** = television

(verb)   (noun)

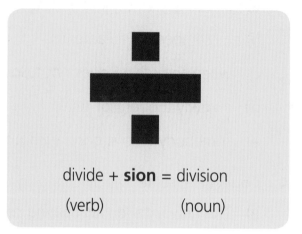

divide + **sion** = division

(verb)   (noun)

Notice that the **se** or **de** ending is removed before adding **–sion**.

Practice activities

1. Change the following verbs into nouns with **–sion** endings.

   explode   _____   erode   _____

   divide   _____   revise   _____

   conclude   _____   decide   _____

   invade   _____   confuse   _____

2. Write some examples of **zhun** and **shun** words in the table below. Include the related verb or noun. Two have been done for you.

zhun sound		*shun* sound	
invade	invasion	act	action

Endings which sound like *zhun*

3. Write the words below in the correct column in the table.

Say the words aloud to help you hear the ending.

extension	permission	evasion
tension	collision	explosion
erosion	admission	vision
procession	intrusion	illusion
decision	profession	mansion

zhun (–sion)	*shun* (–sion)	*shun* (–ssion)

–ship, –hood and –ness endings

Key to spelling

Some suffixes change the meaning of the root word without any requirement for changing the ending of the root word itself. You must, of course, make sure that the word created makes sense.

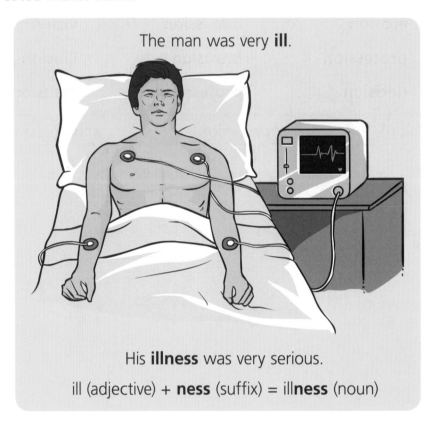

The man was very **ill**.

His **illness** was very serious.

ill (adjective) + **ness** (suffix) = ill**ness** (noun)

Practice activities

1. Make some words by adding the suffixes **–ness**, **–hood** and **–ship**.

–ness		–hood		–ship	
sick		boy		friend	
tired		neighbour		hard	
bright		brother		leader	
gentle		child		fellow	
quiet		parent		scholar	

–ship, –hood and –ness endings

2. The suffixes **–ship**, **–hood** and **–ness** have been mixed up in these words. Write each word correctly in the table below. The first one has been done for you.

sadship	girlness	friendhood
boyship	darkhood	worness
leaderness	coarseship	usefulship
childness	fellowness	carelesshood
sharpship	manness	kinghood

–ship words	–hood words	–ness words
		sadness

Test your spelling

Look at the words.

Say them aloud.

Cover the words.

Write them from memory.

Check your spelling.

shyness	sharpness	darkness
tiredness	boyhood	hardship
childhood	neighbourhood	
friendship	leadership	

Prefixes 1: un–, dis– and mis–

Key to spelling

A **prefix** is a group of letters that may be added to the beginning of a word. When you add a prefix it does not change the spelling of the root word, but it does change its meaning.

| well | **un**well | agree | **dis**agree | behave | **mis**behave |

When you add the prefixes **un–** and **dis–**, they make the word mean the opposite. The prefix **mis–** often means wrong or something done badly.

Practice activities

1. Make some words with prefixes.

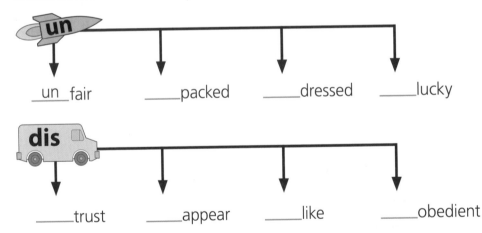

_un_fair   _____packed   _____dressed   _____lucky

_____trust   _____appear   _____like   _____obedient

2. Add the prefix **un–**, **dis–** or **mis–** to the underlined word to change the meaning of each sentence.

   a) I was very _____lucky.

   b) Magicians make rabbits _____appear.

   c) The children were _____behaving.

   d) I _____trust what you say.

   e) I _____like sprouts.

   f) The ball was _____hit.

Prefixes 1: un–, dis– and mis–

3. Add **un–**, **dis–** or **mis–** to these words to change their meaning.

   a) _____tidy

   b) _____guide

   c) _____courage

   d) _____appoint

   e) _____true

   f) _____grace

   g) _____behave

   h) _____pleasant

   i) _____obey

   j) _____lead

   k) _____charge

   l) _____common

   m) _____agree

   n) _____spell

   o) _____healthy

   p) _____grateful

   q) _____appear

Test your spelling

Look at the words.

Say them aloud.

Cover the words.

Write them from memory.

Check your spelling.

unpleasant	disobey	undo
unavoidable	mislead	mishit
disappoint	disappear	
misbehave	misspell	

Prefixes 2: in– and im–

Key to spelling

The prefix **in–** usually means **not**, although it can sometimes also mean **in** or **into**. If the root word starts with **m** or **p**, the prefix changes to **im–**.

expensive   **in**expensive

perfect   **im**perfect

When you add the prefixes **in–** and **im–**, they often make the word which is **opposite** in meaning.

Practice activities

1. Add the prefixes to the root words to give them the opposite meaning.

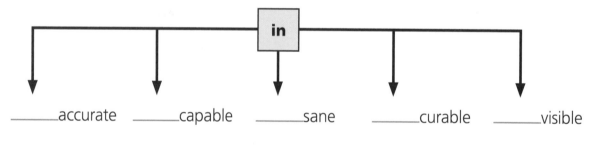

in

_____accurate   _____capable   _____sane   _____curable   _____visible

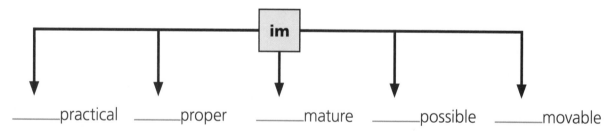

im

_____practical   _____proper   _____mature   _____possible   _____movable

2. Choose **in–** or **im–** to begin each word to give it the opposite meaning.

_____proper   _____capable   _____movable

_____visible   _____practical   _____accurate

Prefixes 2: in– and im–

3. Rewrite each sentence. Add a prefix to the underlined word to give the sentence the opposite meaning.

a) Anna's maths is always <u>accurate</u>.

_____

b) The roses had greenfly – they were <u>perfect</u>.

_____

c) Tom was <u>mature</u> for his age.

_____

d) The man appeared quite <u>sane</u>.

_____

e) Amy was <u>capable</u> of doing better.

_____

f) The idea sounded <u>practical</u>.

_____

g) My new model train was <u>expensive</u>.

_____

h) Most of the answers were <u>correct</u>.

_____

Test your spelling

Look at the words.

Say them aloud.

Cover the words.

Write them from memory.

Check your spelling.

inactive	incorrect	insane
indefinite	indirect	imperfect
immature	impossible	
impatient	immortal	

Prefixes 3: il– and ir–

Key to spelling

If a root word begins with an **l**, then the **in–** prefix changes to **il–**. When the root word begins with **r**, it changes to **ir–**.

legal   **il**legal

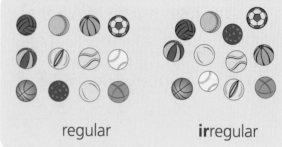

regular   **ir**regular

When you add the prefix **il–** or **ir–**, it often gives the word the **opposite** meaning.

Practice activities

1. Add the prefix **il–** to these words to make them mean the opposite.

    _____legal   _____legible

    _____logical   _____legitimate

    _____literate   _____liberal

2. Take the **ir–** prefix off these words to give them the opposite meaning.

    a) irresponsible   _____

    b) irrelevant   _____

    c) irreverent   _____

    d) irregular   _____

    e) irresistible   _____

    f) irrational   _____

3. Write an **il–** or **ir–** word for each definition below.

Use a dictionary to help you.

a) not legal _____

b) not regular _____

c) not responsible _____

d) not possible to resist _____

e) not legible to read _____

f) not rational or reasonable _____

g) not logical _____

h) not having anything to do with the
subject being discussed _____

i) not being able to read or write _____

j) not legitimate _____

k) having no reverence or respect _____

l) not permitted for moral or
ethical reasons _____

m) not redeemable _____

Test your spelling

Look at the words.

Say them aloud.

Cover the words.

Write them from memory.

Check your spelling.

illegal	illogical	illiterate
illegible	irregular	irrelevant
illegitimate	irresponsible	
irresistible	irrational	

Prefixes 4: A variety of meanings

Key to spelling

Prefixes can have many different meanings. Some, such as **un–** and **dis–**, change the word to its opposite meaning. Here are the meanings of some other prefixes:

re– means 'again' or 'back', e.g. **re**turn.

sub– means 'under', e.g. **sub**side.

inter– means 'between' or 'among', e.g. **inter**lock.

super– means 'above', e.g. **super**sonic.

anti– means 'against', e.g. **anti**bacterial.

auto– means 'self' or 'own', e.g. **auto**pilot.

Practice activities

1. Use the correct prefix to make these words match the definitions.

    a) Between nations   _____national

    b) My own biography   _____biography

    c) Bigger than a small market or shop   _____market

    d) Appear again   _____appear

    e) Preventing becoming septic   _____septic

    f) Happens by itself   _____matic

    g) Related to each other   _____related

    h) Come back   _____turn

    i) Do something again   _____do

    j) An underwater vessel   _____marine

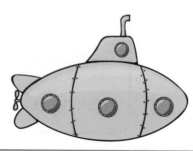

Answers

Pages 4–5
1. bin, leg, cap, hand, mask, twig, pram, clap
2. boat, purse, moon, mouse, light, torch, paint, bird
3. shed, moth, ring, chips, fish, thirty

Pages 6–7
1. **a)** sed/said
   b) beecuz/because
   c) peepul/people
   d) wud/would
   e) muther/mother
   f) litul/little
   g) sanwij/sandwich
2. **a)** shoes **b)** climb **c)** pretty **d)** kind
   e) hour **f)** floor **g)** laugh
3. **a)** could **b)** should **c)** could/would
   d) would **e)** Would **f)** Should **g)** could

Pages 8–9
1. neat, heap, speak, team, beach
2. read, deaf, sweat, weather, meadow
3. food, stool, hoop, proof, broom
4. good, book, foot, stood, shook
5. **a)** cube **b)** rode **c)** ripe **d)** code **e)** pipe
   f) wine **g)** hate **h)** fine **i)** cape **j)** shine
   k) hide **l)** made

Pages 10–11
1. dish/dishes; kiss/kisses; cat/cats;
   coach/coaches; fox/foxes; song/songs;
   boss/bosses; tree/trees; six/sixes;
   catch/catches; bus/buses; miss/misses
2. **a)** dresses **b)** bushes **c)** horse **d)** benches
   e) carpet **f)** windows **g)** bus **h)** pizza
3. **s** – kiss, boss, bus, miss; **x** – fox, six;
   ch – coach, catch; **sh** – dish

Pages 12–13
1. modern 2, invade 2, cabin 2, king 1,
   determine 3, sport 1, together 3,
   introduce 3, industry 3, seat 1, expensive 3,
   September 3, travel 2, habit 2, method 2,
   direct 2, farm 1, bird 1
2. **a)** Monday, Tuesday, Thursday, Friday, Sunday
   b) Wednesday, Saturday

3. **a)** March, May, June
   b) April, July, August
   c) September, October, November, December
   d) January, February
4. 3, 2, 4, 1

Pages 14–15
1. **a)** footstep, footpath, football
   b) snowman, snowstorm, snowflake
   c) sunlight, sunshine, sunshade
   d) rainbow, rainfall, raincoat
   e) handbag, handmade, handkerchief
   f) playground, playtime, playhouse
2. **a)** butter; fly
   b) news; paper
   c) tree; house
   d) bomb; shell
   e) cup; board
   f) door; step
   g) water; fall
   h) goose; berry
   i) waist; coat
3. **a)** bathroom **b)** pancake **c)** saucepan
   d) toothbrush **e)** buttercup **f)** beanstalk

Pages 16–17
1. stir, term, nurse, church
2. play, eight, weigh, sail
3. boiled, soil, loyal, enjoy
4. **a)** their **b)** There **c)** there **d)** their
5. **a)** hear **b)** here **c)** here **d)** hear
6. **a)** too **b)** to **c)** two **d)** too, to **e)** too, to

Pages 18–19
1. hedge, ledge, trudge, budge
2. orange, huge, age, bulge
3. garage, gadget, badge, hedgehog, fudge, wage
   (not kitchen and latch)
4. bridge, dodgem/dodge, village, barge, orange, lodge, badger, hedge

Pages 20–21
1. **a)** right, fight, tight
   b) tire, wire, fire

Answers

c) page, rage, cage
d) clear, hear, dear
e) fetch, sketch, ditch
2. Sentences will vary, but they must contain at least two words with the same ending, e.g. *She could hear them loud and clear.*
3. a) wedge, hedge, sledge
b) hitch, pitch, witch
c) dare, rare, share
d) core, bore, tore
e) blue, glue, clue
f) pie, die, tie
g) foe, doe, roe
h) dire, sire, hire

Pages 22–23

1. jump, garden, call, camp
2. preferred, visited, exclaimed, hovered, occurred, begged
3. a) When I was in Year 1, I always **preferred** to have a hot school dinner.
b) Two years ago, the same argument always **occurred** at the bus stop.
c) The children **begged** for every penny they raised.
d) There is a **limited** range of goods for sale.
e) The teenagers had trouble **admitting** they were wrong.
f) Sunbathing is **relaxing**, but not if it is too hot.
g) All of our class enjoy **gardening** in the school allotment.
h) Tomorrow I will **begin** my homework project.

Pages 24–25

1. a) preparation b) aviation c) imagination
d) admiration e) evaporation f) jubilation
2. suffocation, innovation, exploitation, adoration, temptation, domination
3. create, imagine, educate, inform, prepare, affirm
4. a) dominate b) information c) evaporate
d) associate e) inform f) imagine
g) education h) exterminate i) transport
j) preparation k) imagination l) creation

Pages 26–27

1. suddenly, basically, quickly, economically, slowly, frantically, loudly, dramatically, lovingly, athletically, hopefully, logically
2. glad, cheap, nice, willing, proud, angelic, slow, quick, comic/comical, sad, basic, smart, mad, stupid
3. horribly, possibly, noisy, weary, heavy, humbly, feebly, idly, terribly, lucky, angry, clumsy, gently, comfortably, lazy, merry

Pages 28–29

1. **–sure** words: measure, pleasure, enclosure, leisure, treasure;
–ture words: departure, adventure, furniture, creature, structure
2. **Circle:** teacher, stretcher, pitcher, richer
3. a) mixture b) adventure c) furniture
d) measure e) creature f) pleasure
g) departure h) enclosure i) picture
j) treasure k) treasure l) measure

Pages 30–31

1. mountainous, advantageous, nervous, dangerous, famous, perilous
2. furious, glorious, mysterious, envious, victorious, luxurious
3. **Set A** – The **e** is dropped before adding **–ous**.
Set B – The **u** is dropped from the root word before adding **–ous**.
Set C – The **–le** ending is dropped and **–ulous** is added.
Set D – The **f** is changed to a **v** before adding **–ous**.

Pages 32–33

1. invention, tension, magician, extension, action, completion, electrician, expansion
2. The **t** at the end of the root word is dropped before adding **–ssion**.
3. a) musician b) politician c) exception
d) invention e) mathematician
4. a) The new **extension** was nearing **completion**.
b) The class had a **discussion** about using **expression**.

Answers

c) **Permission** was given for **admission** of infants to the disco.

d) She had an **injection** to release the painful **tension**.

Pages 34–35

1. explosion, erosion, division, revision, conclusion, decision, invasion, confusion

2. Examples of *zhun* sounding words: invade/invasion, explode/explosion, divide/division, erode/erosion, collide/collision, intrude/intrusion, confuse/confusion; Examples of *shun* sounding words: act/action, inflate/inflation, inject/injection, complete/completion, discuss/discussion, permit/permission, extend/extension, tense/tension, electric/electrician, magic/magician

3. *zhun* (–sion): erosion, decision, collision, intrusion, evasion, explosion, vision, illusion
   shun (–sion): extension, tension, mansion
   shun (–ssion): procession, permission, admission, profession

Pages 36–37

1. **–ness** words: sickness, tiredness, brightness, gentleness, quietness
   –hood words: boyhood, neighbourhood, brotherhood, childhood, parenthood
   –ship words: friendship, hardship, leadership, fellowship, scholarship

2. **–ship** words: friendship, worship, leadership, fellowship, kingship;
   –hood words: girlhood, boyhood, childhood, manhood;
   –ness words: sadness, darkness, coarseness, usefulness, carelessness, sharpness

Pages 38–39

1. **un–**: unfair, unpacked, undressed, unlucky
   dis–: distrust, disappear, dislike, disobedient

2. a) **un**lucky b) **dis**appear c) **mis**behaving
   d) **dis**trust e) **dis**like f) **mis**hit

3. a) **un**tidy b) **mis**guide c) **dis**courage
   d) **dis**appoint e) **un**true f) **dis**grace
   g) **mis**behave h) **un**pleasant

i) **dis**obey j) **mis**lead k) **dis**charge
l) **un**common m) **dis**agree n) **mis**spell
o) **un**healthy p) **un**grateful
q) **dis**appear

Pages 40–41

1. **in–:** inaccurate, incapable, insane, incurable, invisible
   im–: impractical, improper, immature, impossible, immovable

2. **im**proper, **in**capable, **im**movable, **in**visible, **im**practical, **in**accurate

3. a) Anna's maths is always **inaccurate**.
   b) The roses had greenfly – they were **imperfect**.
   c) Tom was **immature** for his age.
   d) The man appeared quite **insane**.
   e) Amy was **incapable** of doing better.
   f) The idea sounded **impractical**.
   g) My new model train was **inexpensive**.
   h) Most of the answers were **incorrect**.

Pages 42–43

1. illegal, illegible, illogical, illegitimate, illiterate, illiberal

2. a) responsible b) relevant c) reverent
   d) regular e) resistible f) rational

3. a) illegal b) irregular c) irresponsible
   d) irresistible e) illegible f) irrational
   g) illogical h) irrelevant i) illiterate
   j) illegitimate k) irreverent l) illicit
   m) irredeemable

Pages 44–45

1. a) **inter**national b) **auto**biography
   c) **super**market d) **re**appear
   e) **anti**septic f) **auto**matic g) **inter**related
   h) **re**turn i) **re**do j) **sub**marine

2. a) superman b) return c) automatic
   d) antidote e) intercity f) submerge

3. a)–f) A range of words are possible, many from pages 44–45. Check responses using a dictionary.

Pages 46–47

1. always, almost, alone, already, also, although

Answers

2. comical, personal, seasonal, accidental, national, ornamental, coastal, logical, classical

3. a) origin b) tropic c) accident d) occasion e) centre f) continent g) nature h) tribe i) crime j) universe k) industry l) choir m) magic n) electric o) fiction

Pages 48–49

1. invent/prevent; sailing/sailor; telephone/microphone; helping/helpless; farmer/farmyard; unclear/clearly; today/daylight; comforting/uncomfortable; builder/building; become/newcomer; unknown/knowledge

2. dislike/unlike; unhappy; refill; refix/unfix; misbehave

3. dished; treatment/treating/treatable/treated; remarked/remarking/remarkable; mixed/mixing/mixture; colouring/coloured/colourful/colourless; boarding/boarder/boarded

Pages 50–51

1. a) The consonant is doubled before adding **–ing**.
   b) Change the **y** to an **i** before adding **–ness**.
   c) If the adjective ends with a **consonant + y**, change the **y** to **i** before adding **–ly**.
   d) When the noun ends in a **consonant + y**, the **y** is changed to **i** before adding **–ous**.

2. a) entertainment b) clearly c) education d) invasion e) forgetting f) dangerous g) departure h) wrestling
   Sentences will vary, but they must contain the stated word with the correct spelling, be correctly punctuated and must make sense.

Pages 52–53

1. a) drive/drove
   b) go/went
   c) sing/sang
   d) find/found
   e) write/wrote
   f) know/knew
   g) hurt/hurt
   h) see/saw
   i) speak/spoke
   j) steal/stole

2. a) I **taught** my dog some tricks.
   b) My parents **gave** me some pocket money.
   c) They **left** at seven o'clock.
   d) We **swam** in the sea.
   e) Ben **hid** from Amy.
   f) I **grew** vegetables in my garden.
   g) Sam **was** often late.
   h) Mrs Jones **felt** ill.

Pages 54–55

1. a) **a**cross b) **be**tween c) **a**bout d) **a**round e) **be**low f) **a**bove g) **a**board h) **a**mong i) **be**yond j) **be**neath k) **a**gainst l) **be**hind

2. a)–i) Sentences will vary, but they must contain the stated word with the correct spelling, be correctly punctuated and must make sense.

Pages 56–57

1. leaf/leaves; half/halves; thief/thieves; shelf/shelves; knife/knives; wife/wives; wolf/wolves; calf/calves; life/lives; elf/elves

2. a) loaves b) knives c) wolves d) shelves e) thieves f) lives g) calves h) wives i) halves

Pages 58–59

1. keys, lorries, trolleys, toys, guys, berries, cries, pulleys

2. fly, boy, copy, lady, day, body, cherry, turkey

3. a) All **turkeys** gobble.
   b) London and Paris are **cities**.
   c) There were two **donkeys** in the field.
   d) We picked some **berries** off the bush.
   e) **Cherries** have stones in them.
   f) Some **trolleys** were outside the supermarket.
   g) **Babies** often cry.

Answers

h) I made two **copies** of the letter.

i) Smoke was coming out of the **chimneys**.

Pages 60–61

1. **a)** volcanoes **b)** potatoes **c)** tomatoes
    d) cargoes **e)** echoes **f)** heroes
2. **a)** pianos **b)** banjos **c)** solos **d)** sopranos
3. **a)** radios **b)** videos **c)** infernos **d)** cameos
    e) folios **f)** ghettos/ghettoes

Pages 62–63

1. lady's, horse's, magician's, children's, child's, countries', churches', church's, girls', boy's, driver's, crew's, squirrels', galleries'
2. **a)** The **ladies'** house.
    b) The **mouse's** cheese.
    c) The **mice's** cheese.
    d) The **boy's** toy.
    e) The **girls'** swing.
    f) The **families'** lake.
    g) The **children's** cakes.
    h) The **goats'** field.
    i) The **troll's** bridge.

Pages 64–65

1. crystal, cymbal, Egypt, hymn, mystery, oxygen, typical
2. **a)** gym **b)** syrup **c)** symbol **d)** myth
    e) hymn
3. **a)** mystery **b)** syllable **c)** pyramids, Egyptians **d)** cymbal **e)** oxygen **f)** system
    g) lyric
4. w**i**nter, **i**nfant, m**y**th, s**i**lly, cr**y**stal, c**y**l**i**nder

Pages 66–67

1. **u words:** umbrella, butter, fund, supply
    ou words: encourage, cousin, nourish, touch
2. y**ou**ng, s**u**pper, tr**ou**ble, c**ou**ntry, th**u**nder
3. **Across:** couple, country, rough
    Down: courage, young
4. **a)–d)** Sentences will vary, but they must contain one of the stated words with the correct spelling, be correctly punctuated and must make sense.

Pages 68–69

1. vein, weigh, obey, eight, freight, hey, prey, veil, survey, they, sleigh, grey, reign, neighbour, convey, reins
2. **a)** great, prey
    b) veil, face
    c) They, cake
    d) always, obey
    e) Eight, place
    f) say, age
    g) survey, late
    h) neighbour, grey
3. **a)–d)** Sentences will vary, but they must contain the stated word with the correct spelling, be correctly punctuated and must make sense.

Pages 70–71

1. **a:** wander, wasp, watch, wash
    o: wobble, worry, womb, woman
2. **a)** woman **b)** wobble **c)** womb **d)** wasp
    e) watch
3. **a)** w**a**rm **b)** sw**a**rm **c)** w**o**rld **d)** w**o**rse
    e) w**a**r **f)** w**o**rk **g)** w**o**rth **h)** w**o**rd
    i) w**o**rm **j)** w**a**rn

Pages 72–73

1. guest, vague, plague, rogue, catalogue, guide, guitar, disguise, guinea, guilty
2. **a)** vague – uncertain or unclear
    b) rogue – a dishonest or mischievous person
    c) catalogue – a list or record of items
    d) disguise – something that changes the appearance of someone, so they cannot be recognised
3. **a)–d)** Sentences will vary, but they must contain the stated word with the correct spelling, be correctly punctuated and make sense.
4. gift, gear, get, gelding, give, giggle, girl, girder, geyser, geese, giddy

Pages 74–75

1. *k* **sound:** school, stomach, character, anchor, chemist, ache, Christmas, architect;

Answers

sh sound: brochure, chef, machine, moustache, parachute, chauffeur, champagne
2. machine, anchor, chemist, chalet, moustache, chorus, brochure, chef
3. **a)** school **b)** Christmas **c)** character
   d) chorus **e)** champagne **f)** chauffeur
   g) machine **h)** anchor **i)** chef **j)** chemist

Pages 76–77
1. tongue, technique, synagogue, colleague, boutique
2. **a)** league – a group of teams or organisations competing or working together
   b) antique – something old, from the past
   c) unique – the only one of its kind
3. bouti**que**, opa**que**, collea**gue**, intri**gue**, mos**que**, ton**gue**, techni**que**, lea**gue**, fati**gue**, uni**que**, va**gue**, anti**que**
4. **a)** plague – a widespread disease or infestation
   b) plaque – a decorative or informative flat plate; a coating on teeth due to the presence of bacteria

Pages 78–79
1. **Across:** science, conscious, muscle
   Down: scent, fascinate, disciple, scenic
2. **a)–i)** Sentences will vary, but they must contain the stated word with the correct spelling, be correctly punctuated and must make sense.

Pages 80–81
1. accept/except; ball/bawl; not/knot; allowed/aloud; hear/here; plain/plane
2. **a)** knows **b)** heal **c)** fair **d)** great
   e) accept **f)** meddle
3. **a)–n)** Sentences will vary, but they must contain the stated word with the correct spelling, be correctly punctuated and must make sense.

Pages 82–83
1. Answers will vary, but could include:
   a) conscious, unconscious
   b) certainly, uncertain

c) surrounded, surrounding
   d) discovered, discovery, discoverer, discovering, undiscovered
   e) describing, description, indescribable
   f) behaviour, behaving, behaved, misbehave
   g) information, informal, misinform
   h) careless, careful, caring
   i) befriend, friendly, friendship, unfriendly
2. **a)–h)** Sentences will vary, but they must contain the stated word with the correct spelling, be correctly punctuated and must make sense.

Pages 84–85
1. **a)** rhythm **b)** island **c)** people
2. **a)–d)** Answers will vary.

Pages 87–88
Note to parent: For each test, read the word, then the word within a sentence, then repeat the word a third time. You should leave at least a 12-second gap between spellings.

Test 1
1. The word is **jump**. I can **jump** very high. The word is **jump**.
2. The word is **push**. The car needed a **push** this morning. The word is **push**.
3. The word is **hedge**. There is a nest in the **hedge**. The word is **hedge**.
4. The word is **station**. The **station** platform was very busy. The word is **station**.
5. The word is **myth**. The storyteller told us the **myth** of the dragon. The word is **myth**.
6. The word is **beginning**. It was **beginning** to snow outside. The word is **beginning**.
7. The word is **misbehave**. Do not **misbehave** during assembly. The word is **misbehave**.
8. The word is **dramatically**. The footballer fell **dramatically**. The word is **dramatically**.
9. The word is **Science**. **Science** is everywhere around us. The word is **Science**.

Answers

10. The word is **various**. There are **various** people at the swimming gala. The word is **various**.

Test 2

1. The word is **step**. Be careful not to trip over the **step**. The word is **step**.
2. The word is **their**. Soon they would arrive at **their** destination. The word is **their**.
3. The word is **castle**. A moat surrounded the **castle**. The word is **castle**.
4. The word is **hopeless**. It was **hopeless** trying to fly the kite. The word is **hopeless**.
5. The word is **young**. Many **young** people like using computers. The word is **young**.
6. The word is **irresponsible**. It is **irresponsible** to throw stones. The word is **irresponsible**.
7. The word is **neighbour**. They made a meal for their elderly **neighbour**. The word is **neighbour**.
8. The word is **politician**. The **politician** promised he would help people. The word is **politician**.
9. The word is **accept**. She could not **accept** the gift. The word is **accept**.
10. The word is **remember**. I tried to **remember** the wizard's name. The word is **remember**.

Test 3

1. The word is **knight**. The **knight** rescued the maiden from the monster. The word is **knight**.
2. The word is **door**. Please close the **door** behind you. The word is **door**.
3. The word is **bridge**. They walked across the **bridge**. The word is **bridge**.
4. The word is **forgotten**. I have **forgotten** my PE kit. The word is **forgotten**.

5. The word is **happily**. They lived **happily** in the enchanted forest. The word is **happily**.
6. The word is **league**. Her favourite team was top of the **league**. The word is **league**.
7. The word is **wolves**. A pack of **wolves** surrounded the man. The word is **wolves**.
8. The word is **rhythm**. Everybody moved to the **rhythm** of the music. The word is **rhythm**.
9. The word is **brochure**. The family looked through the holiday **brochure**. The word is **brochure**.
10. The word is **disguise**. The sunglasses were a **disguise**. The word is **disguise**.

Test 4

1. The word is **said**. Everybody **said** the bride looked pretty. The word is **said**.
2. The word is **truly**. He was **truly** sorry for the mess he had made. The word is **truly**.
3. The word is **famous**. They recognised the lady as a **famous** actress. The word is **famous**.
4. The word is **typical**. It was a **typical** wet day. The word is **typical**.
5. The word is **eight**. They were just **eight** miles from home. The word is **eight**.
6. The word is **warm**. It was a lovely **warm** day. The word is **warm**.
7. The word is **because**. I will go **because** I want to. The word is **because**.
8. The word is **potatoes**. We often have **potatoes** at school. The word is **potatoes**.
9. The word is **confusion**. Much **confusion** was caused by the loud bang. The word is **confusion**.
10. The word is **enormous**. The cruise ship was **enormous**. The word is **enormous**.

Answers

Prefixes 4: A variety of meanings

2. Match the prefix to the root word. The first one has been done for you.

    a) super   dote

    b) re   city

    c) auto   turn

    d) anti   man

    e) inter   merge

    f) sub   matic

3. Write as many words as you can find for each prefix.

    Use a dictionary to help you.

    a) re– _____

    b) sub– _____

    c) inter– _____

    d) super– _____

    e) anti– _____

    f) auto– _____

Test your spelling

Look at the words.

Say them aloud.

Cover the words.

Write them from memory.

Check your spelling.

redo	superstar	submerge
interact	international	reappear
interrelated	antiseptic	
automatic	autograph	

45

Adding al to words

The letters **al** may be used as either a prefix or a suffix to change the meaning of words.

al + one

alone

music + al

music**al**

Take care! When you use **al** as a prefix or a suffix, you only use one **l**.

Practice activities

1. Make some words by adding the prefix **al–**.

    _____ways   _____most   _____one

    _____ready   _____so   _____though

2. Change these nouns into adjectives by adding the suffix **–al**.

    comic_____   person_____   season_____

    accident_____   nation_____   ornament_____

    coast_____   logic_____   classic_____

3. Take the **–al** suffix off each of these adjectives. Write the root word you are left with.

Use a dictionary if necessary. Take care! Sometimes the spelling of the root word has been slightly changed.

a) original   _____

b) tropical   _____

c) accidental   _____

d) occasional   _____

e) central   _____

f) continental   _____

g) natural   _____

h) tribal   _____

i) criminal   _____

j) universal   _____

k) industrial   _____

l) choral   _____

m) magical   _____

n) electrical   _____

o) fictional   _____

Test your spelling

Look at the words.

Say them aloud.

Cover the words.

Write them from memory.

Check your spelling.

also	always	almost
already	although	comical
musical	seasonal	
natural	economical	

Common roots

Key to spelling

Being able to identify the root word can sometimes help you with spelling.

to**day**

daylight

Practice activities

1. Match up the pairs of words that contain the same root words. Underline the common root word in both. The first one has been done for you.

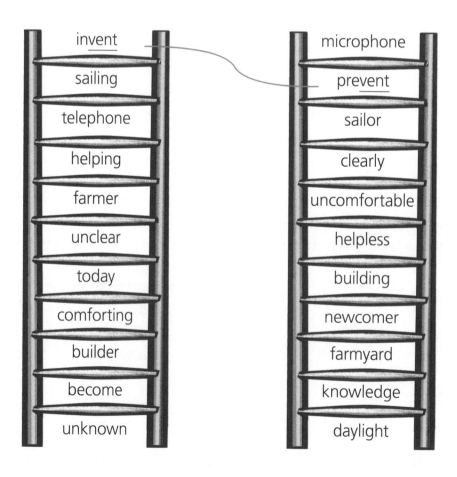

invent	microphone
sailing	prevent
telephone	sailor
helping	clearly
farmer	uncomfortable
unclear	helpless
today	building
comforting	newcomer
builder	farmyard
become	knowledge
unknown	daylight

Common roots

2. Add a prefix to each root word to make a longer word. The first one has been done for you.

root word	prefix + root word
like	dislike
happy	
fill	
fix	
behave	

3. Add a suffix to each root word to make a longer word. Avoid plural versions of the words. The first one has been done for you.

root word	root word + suffix
dish	dished
treat	
remark	
mix	
colour	
board	

Test your spelling

Look at the words.

Say them aloud.

Cover the words.

Write them from memory.

Check your spelling.

outside	sideline	display
player	discovery	recovered
drinking	undrinkable	
good	goodness	

Common mistakes

When prefixes and suffixes have been applied, it is quite common for the root word to be misspelt. If these words are thought of in terms of root words and the rules for adding prefixes and suffixes are then applied, the words are less likely to be misspelt.

disappear
(just add **dis–** to **appear**)

disappoint
(just add **dis–** to **appoint**)

Remember that many suffixes require the root word to be changed.

Practice activities

1. Look at the word pairs below. Write a rule for adding the suffix to the root word.

    a) begin   beginn**ing**

    _____

    b) busy   busi**ness**

    _____

    c) necessary   necessari**ly**

    _____

    d) glory   glori**ous**

    _____

2. Change each root word by adding the given suffix. Write a sentence containing each word.

a) entertain (ment)

_____

b) clear (ly)

_____

c) educate (tion)

_____

d) invade (sion)

_____

e) forget (ing)

_____

f) danger (ous)

_____

g) depart (ure)

_____

h) wrestle (ing)

_____

Test your spelling

Look at the words.

Say them aloud.

Cover the words.

Write them from memory.

Check your spelling.

mysterious	glorious	business
disappear	departing	beginning
forgetting	necessary	
necessarily	unnecessary	

The past tense of irregular verbs

Key to spelling

The spelling of the past tense of irregular verbs is sometimes surprising and does not follow a clear pattern.

caught
The girl ~~catched~~ a cold.

catch (verb)
caught (past tense)

wore
The boy ~~weared~~ his new trainers.

wear (verb)
wore (past tense)

Practice activities

1. Match up the present tense of each verb with its past tense. The first one has been done for you.

present tense	past tense
a) drive	sang
b) go	knew
c) sing	drove
d) find	hurt
e) write	went
f) know	wrote
g) hurt	spoke
h) see	found
i) speak	stole
j) steal	saw

The past tense of irregular verbs

2. Change the underlined irregular verb into the past tense and rewrite the sentence. The first one has been done for you.

a) I <u>teach</u> my dog some tricks.

   I **taught** my dog some tricks.

b) My parents <u>give</u> me some pocket money.

c) They <u>leave</u> at seven o'clock.

d) We <u>swim</u> in the sea.

e) Ben <u>hides</u> from Amy.

f) I <u>grow</u> vegetables in my garden.

g) Sam <u>is</u> often late.

h) Mrs Jones <u>feels</u> ill.

Test your spelling

Look at the words.

Say them aloud.

Cover the words.

Write them from memory.

Check your spelling.

taught	knew	gave
chose	bought	rode
left	forgot	
began	ate	

Prepositions

Key to spelling

Prepositions appear frequently in our writing. They show you how one thing relates to another.

The boy is hiding **under** the table.

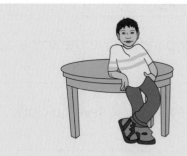

The boy is leaning **against** the table.

Practice activities

1. Make prepositions by adding **a–** or **be–** before each of the following. Rewrite the new word. The first one has been done for you.

   Use a dictionary to check your answers.

   a) cross   across

   b) tween   _____

   c) bout   _____

   d) round   _____

   e) low   _____

   f) bove   _____

   g) board   _____

   h) mong   _____

   i) yond   _____

   j) neath   _____

   k) gainst   _____

   l) hind   _____

2. Write a sentence containing the given preposition. The first one has been done for you.

a) from

A postcard came **from** their friends.

b) near

_____

c) after

_____

d) against

_____

e) above

_____

f) under

_____

g) through

_____

h) towards

_____

i) beneath

_____

Test your spelling

Look at the words.

Say them aloud.

Cover the words.

Write them from memory.

Check your spelling.

along	across	above
around	below	between
before	outside	
under	near	

Plural of f and fe endings

Key to spelling

When a noun ends with **f** or **fe**, you usually change the **f** or **fe** to **v** and add **es** to make it plural.

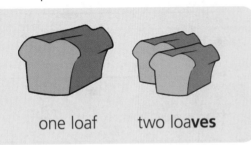

one loaf   two loa**ves**

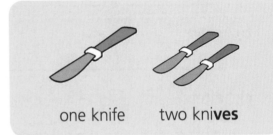

one knife   two kni**ves**

Be careful – words do not always follow the rules!

chief – chie**fs**   roof – roo**fs**   hoof – hoo**fs**   dwarf – dwar**fs**

Practice activities

1. Complete the table. The first one has been done for you.

singular	plural
leaf	leaves
half	
thief	
shelf	
knife	
	wives
	wolves
	calves
	lives
	elves

Plural of f and fe endings

2. Complete these sentences by using the correct form of the plural in each gap.

a) The baker made lots of _____ (loaf).

b) We use _____ (knife) to cut things.

c) A pack of _____ (wolf) lives in the woods.

d) I have lots of _____ (shelf) in my room.

e) Some _____ (thief) broke into the shop.

f) Does a cat have nine _____ (life)?

g) The cow has two _____ (calf).

h) The two _____ (wife) were good friends.

i) In a football match there are two _____ (half).

Test your spelling

Look at the words.

Say them aloud.

Cover the words.

Write them from memory.

Check your spelling.

leaves	halves	shelves
thieves	knives	wives
loaves	wolves	
calves	lives	

Plural of y endings

When a noun ends with a **vowel + y**, you usually add **s** to make it plural.

one monkey   two monkey**s**

When a noun ends with a **consonant + y**, you change the **y** to **i** and add **es**.

one baby   two bab**ies**

Practice activities

1. Write the plural of these nouns.

    key   _____   lorry   _____

    trolley   _____   toy   _____

    guy   _____   berry   _____

    cry   _____   pulley   _____

2. Write the singular of these nouns.

    flies   _____   boys   _____

    copies   _____   ladies   _____

    days   _____   bodies   _____

    cherries   _____   turkeys   _____

3. Rewrite these sentences correctly.

Each sentence contains one spelling mistake.

a) All turkies gobble.

_____

b) London and Paris are citys.

_____

c) There were two donkies in the field.

_____

d) We picked some berrys off the bush.

_____

e) Cherrys have stones in them.

_____

f) Some trollies were outside the supermarket.

_____

g) Babys often cry.

_____

h) I made two copys of the letter.

_____

i) Smoke was coming out of the chimnies.

_____

Test your spelling

Look at the words.

Say them aloud.

Cover the words.

Write them from memory.

Check your spelling.

valleys	guys	kidneys
toys	holidays	skies
ferries	poppies	
enemies	diaries	

Plural of words ending in o

Key to spelling

You need to learn the rules for spelling the plural of nouns ending in **o**. Always check in a dictionary if you are not sure.

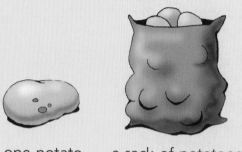

one potato   a sack of potato**es**

Rule 1

Many common nouns ending in a **consonant + o** add **es** in the plural.

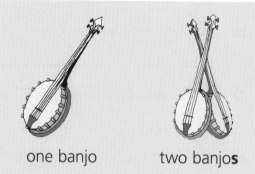

one banjo   two banjo**s**

Rule 2

Some words ending with **o** just add **s**, e.g. less familiar words, **foreign words** or words that end with a **vowel + o**.

Practice activities

1. Use the plural form of the noun in brackets to complete each sentence.
    The nouns all follow Rule 1.

    a) In the distance we saw some _____ (volcano) erupting.

    b) I like _____ (potato) more than carrots.

    c) We picked some _____ (tomato) for our tea.

    d) The ships carried _____ (cargo) of gold and silver.

    e) When we shouted we heard the _____ (echo) of our voices.

    f) The soldiers were _____ (hero) in the war.

Plural of words ending in o

2. Use Rule 2 to help you write the plural form of these nouns. They are all connected with music. The nouns originally come from another language.

a) piano _____

b) banjo _____

c) solo _____

d) soprano _____

The plural of solo is spelt the same backwards or forwards!

3. Write the plural of each of these words.

a) radio _____

b) video _____

c) inferno _____

d) cameo _____

e) folio _____

f) ghetto _____

Test your spelling

Look at the words.

Say them aloud.

Cover the words.

Write them from memory.

Check your spelling.

potatoes	tomatoes	radios
infernos	videos	pianos
echoes	heroes	
solos	volcanoes	

The possessive apostrophe

Key to spelling

The possessive apostrophe shows that something is possessed by somebody or something else.

The boy's book.
The book belongs to the boy.

The girls' swimming pool.
The swimming pool belongs to both girls.

For all singular, and most plural, nouns the apostrophe and **s** is added to the end of the word, e.g. the dog's bowl, the children's playroom.

If the noun is a plural already ending with **s**, then just the apostrophe is added, e.g. the girls' football team, the boys' changing rooms.

Practice activities

1. Change each word by rewriting it with the possessive apostrophe, adding **s** where necessary. The first one has been done for you.

lady	lady's	**horse**	_____
magician	_____	**children**	_____
child	_____	**countries**	_____
churches	_____	**church**	_____
girls	_____	**boy**	_____
driver	_____	**crew**	_____
squirrels	_____	**galleries**	_____

The possessive apostrophe

2. Rewrite the sentences using the possessive apostrophe for the underlined words. The first one has been done for you.

    a) The house belonging to three ladies.

        The **ladies'** house.

    b) The cheese belonging to one mouse.

        _____

    c) The cheese belonging to three mice.

        _____

    d) The toy belonging to one boy.

        _____

    e) The swing belonging to two girls.

        _____

    f) The lake belonging to four families.

        _____

    g) The cakes belonging to seven children.

        _____

    h) The field belonging to three goats.

        _____

    i) The bridge belonging to one troll.

        _____

Test your spelling

Look at the words.

Say them aloud.

Cover the words.

Write them from memory.

Check your spelling.

children's	boys'	girls'
mice's	hero's	heroes'
ladies'	men's	
magician's	families'	

Using y to spell the short *i* sound

Key to spelling

Sometimes the short *i* sound (as in p**i**g) is spelt using a **y**.

hymn

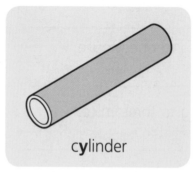
c**y**linder

g**y**m

These do not follow a rule. You just have to become familiar with words containing this spelling.

Practice activities

1. Rewrite the list of words in alphabetical order.

mystery _____

typical _____

crystal _____

hymn _____

Egypt _____

oxygen _____

cymbal _____

2. Correct the following words by rewriting them using a **y** for the short *i* sound.

a) gim _____

b) sirup _____

c) simbol _____

d) mith _____

e) himn _____

64

Using y to spell the short *i* sound

3. Complete each sentence with the correct word from the list below.

Use a dictionary if you are unsure of the meaning of any of the words.

mystery	lyric	cymbal	system
oxygen	pyramids	syllable	Egyptians

a) Nobody knew how to solve the _____ of the missing diamond.

b) Each beat in a spoken word is called a _____.

c) The _____ were built by the ancient _____.

d) The drumstick broke when the drummer struck the _____.

e) The gas _____ is essential for animals to breathe.

f) At the centre of the solar _____ is the Sun.

g) She could not get the song _____ out of her head.

4. Decide whether a **y** or **i** should be inserted into each space to make the short *i* sound.

Use a dictionary to check whether you have chosen correctly.

w__nter   __nfant   m__th

s__lly   cr__stal   c__l__nder

Test your spelling

Look at the words.

Say them aloud.

Cover the words.

Write them from memory.

Check your spelling.

myth	gym	Egypt
pyramid	mystery	oxygen
symbol	crystal	
typical	hymn	

When ou spells the *u* sound

Key to spelling

Some words in which you hear the short *u* sound (as in m**u**g) use the spelling **ou**.

double   couple

country

This is another spelling which just has to be learned. There is no rule, so you have to remember words which are spelt in this way.

Practice activities

1. Complete the table by writing words from the list into the correct column.

    umbrella   encourage   cousin   butter
    fund   nourish   supply   touch

u words	ou words

2. Complete the following words with either **ou** or **u**.

    Check using a dictionary.

    y____ng   s____pper   tr____ble   c____ntry   th____nder

When ou spells the *u* sound

3. Fill in the white squares to complete the words.

			c			p	l	e
	c			n	t	r	y	
			r					
			a					
r			g	h			n	
			e				g	

4. Write sentences containing at least one from each pair of words.

a) cousin, young

_____

b) trouble, rough

_____

c) courage, touch

_____

d) couple, country

_____

Test your spelling

Look at the words.

Say them aloud.

Cover the words.

Write them from memory.

Check your spelling.

young	cousin	double
trouble	couple	country
rough	touch	
enough	courage	

Words with ei, eigh and ey

Key to spelling

The letter patterns **ei**, **eigh** and **ey** often make the long **a** sound, as in g**a**me.

How much do I w**eigh**?

Eight balls

There is no rule for these spelling patterns. They just have to be learned.

Practice activities

1. Underline the words in which **ei**, **eigh** or **ey** make the long **a** sound.

   Be careful – some words are included to trick you!

vein	play	state	weigh
day	obey	eight	height
foray	freight	hey	prey
clay	delay	veil	snail
survey	their	rate	they
sleigh	grey	rain	reign
neighbour	convey	reins	holiday

Words with ei, eigh and ey

2. Identify and write two words containing the long **a** sound in each of these sentences.

   a) The great beast stalked his prey. _____ _____

   b) The veil covered the bride's face. _____ _____

   c) They eat their cake at lunchtime. _____ _____

   d) You must always obey the rules. _____ _____

   e) Eight girls liked the place. _____ _____

   f) Some say 'age before beauty'. _____ _____

   g) The survey was finished late. _____ _____

   h) The neighbour had grey hair. _____ _____

3. Write sentences containing each of these words.

   a) weigh

   _____

   b) vein

   _____

   c) they

   _____

   d) neighbour

   _____

Test your spelling

Look at the words.

Say them aloud.

Cover the words.

Write them from memory.

Check your spelling.

vein	weigh	eight
they	obey	grey
eighth	survey	
veil	neighbour	

Words with wa and wo

Key to spelling

The vowels **a** and **o** do not behave as expected after the letter **w**.

a swan in a swamp

The letter **a** is often pronounced like an **o** when it comes after **w**.

a wonderful wolf

The letter **o** may be pronounced in several different ways after **w**.

Practice activities

1. Make some words by inserting **a** or **o**. One has been done for you.

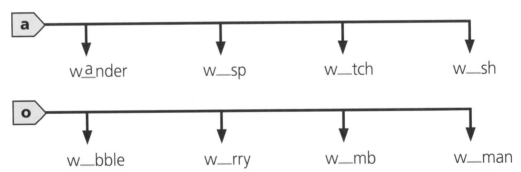

w_a_nder   w__sp   w__tch   w__sh

w__bble   w__rry   w__mb   w__man

2. Write the **wa** or **wo** word which means:

   a) the opposite of man   _____

   b) to rock unsteadily   _____

   c) the place where a baby grows   _____

   d) a flying insect that stings   _____

   e) like a small clock   _____

Words with wa and wo

*When **ar** comes after **w** it often sounds like **or**.*

*When **or** comes after **w** it often sounds like **er**.*

3. Choose **ar** or **or** to complete each word, using the clues to help you.

Use a dictionary if necessary.

    a) w_____m   quite hot

    b) sw_____m   a large number of insects

    c) w_____ld   the Earth

    d) w_____se   less good

    e) w_____   a conflict between countries

    f) w_____k   a job

    g) w_____th   to have a certain value

    h) w_____d   a group of letters

    i) w_____m   lives in the soil

    j) w_____n   to tell someone of danger

Test your spelling

Look at the words.

Say them aloud.

Cover the words.

Write them from memory.

Check your spelling.

wasp	**watch**	**woman**
wombat	**wonder**	**worm**
work	**word**	
warm	**reward**	

Words with gu

Key to spelling

The letter **g** usually makes a hard sound in words (as in **g**ate and **g**o). To keep its hard sound, you often put **u** after **g** when it comes before **e** or **i**.

guess

guitar

Practice activities

1. Make some words using **gu**. The first one has been done for you.

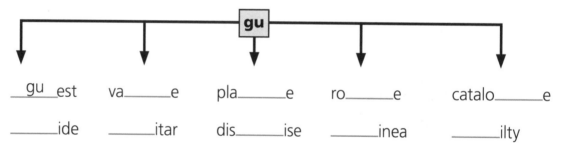

gu___est   va_____e   pla_____e   ro_____e   catalo_____e

_____ide   _____itar   dis_____ise   _____inea   _____ilty

2. Write the meaning of the words below.

   Use a dictionary to help you.

   a) vague

   _____

   b) rogue

   _____

   c) catalogue

   _____

   d) disguise

   _____

3. Use the following words correctly in sentences of your own.

    a) league

    _____

    b) tongue

    _____

    c) intrigue

    _____

    d) dialogue

    _____

4. Underline the words that do not follow the **gu** rule.

gift	vague	gear	get
plague	gelding	guest	give
giggle	catalogue	rogue	girl
guilty	girder	league	geyser
geese	guitar	giddy	tongue

Look at the words.

Say them aloud.

Cover the words.

Write them from memory.

Check your spelling.

guess	guest	guilty
guide	guitar	rogue
league	disguise	
vague	guillotine	

ch from different languages

Key to spelling

English uses lots of spellings from different languages.

Sometimes the **k** sound (as in **k**it) is spelt **ch**.

Christmas

This spelling originates from Greek.

Sometimes the **sh** sound (as in **sh**op) is spelt **ch**.

chef

This spelling often has French origins.

Practice activities

1. Rewrite the **ch** words in the correct column of the table.

   brochure   school   stomach   character   chef

   anchor   machine   chemist   ache   Christmas

   moustache   parachute   chauffeur   champagne   architect

ch making a *k* sound	ch making a *sh* sound

74

ch from different languages

2. Rewrite each word with the correct spelling.

mashine _____   ankor _____

kemist _____   shalet _____

moustashe _____   korus _____

broshure _____   shef _____

3. Write the correct **ch** word for each definition.

Check your answers using a dictionary.

a) Where children are educated. _____

b) The festival celebrating the birth of Christ. _____

c) A person in a book or a film. _____

d) Part of a song. _____

e) An expensive sparkling wine. _____

f) Somebody who drives people around. _____

g) A mechanical tool for making things. _____

h) A heavy object to stop a ship floating away. _____

i) Sometimes referred to as a cook. _____

j) A person who experiments with chemicals. _____

Test your spelling

Look at the words.

Say them aloud.

Cover the words.

Write them from memory.

Check your spelling.

chorus	anchor	machine
chauffeur	school	chemist
Christmas	brochure	
character	chef	

–gue and –que from French

Key to spelling

Many English words and spellings originate from France.

Words ending with a **g** sound (as in **g**ap) are sometimes spelt with a **–gue** ending.

fati**gue**

Words ending with a **k** sound (as in **k**id) are sometimes spelt with a **–que** ending.

mos**que**

Practice activities

1. Using the sounds described above, underline the words that might have a French origin.

   ring   tongue   technique   synagogue

   kick   colleague   hog   boutique

2. Write a definition for each of the words below.

   Use a dictionary to help you.

   a) league

   _____

   b) antique

   _____

   c) unique

   _____

–gue and –que from French

3. Choose **–gue** or **–que** to complete each word.

   Use a dictionary to check your spelling.

   bouti_____   opa_____
   collea_____   intri_____
   mos_____   ton_____
   techni_____   lea_____
   fati_____   uni_____
   va_____   anti_____

4. Both **–gue** and **–que** can be added to **pla–** to make the words **plague** or **plaque**. Write down the meaning of each of these words.

   a) plague

   _____

   _____

   b) plaque

   _____

   _____

Test your spelling

Look at the words.

Say them aloud.

Cover the words.

Write them from memory.

Check your spelling.

league	antique	colleague
synagogue	unique	tongue
mosque	plague	
plaque	technique	

Spelling the *s* sound with sc

Key to spelling

It is not uncommon for the **s** sound (as in **s**at) to be spelt **sc**. This spelling comes from Latin and the Romans probably said **sc** with the **s** followed by a **k** sound, as in **sk**y. It may help you to spell **sc** words by remembering this.

scene

scissors

Practice activities

1. Fill in the white squares to complete the words.

		f						
		a						
		s			e	n	c	e
					d			
	o	n	s	c	i	o		
e		a						c
n		t						e
t		e			i			n
					p			i
	m	u					e	c
					e			

Spelling the *s* sound with sc

2. Write a sentence containing the given **sc** word.

   Use a dictionary if you are unsure of the meaning of the word.

   a) muscles

   _____

   b) scissors

   _____

   c) science

   _____

   d) fascinating

   _____

   e) descend

   _____

   f) unconscious

   _____

   g) scent

   _____

   h) crescent

   _____

   i) scene

   _____

Test your spelling

Look at the words.

Say them aloud.

Cover the words.

Write them from memory.

Check your spelling.

science	scene	scissors
disciple	muscle	fascinate
conscious	crescent	
descend	scent	

Sounds familiar!

Homophones are words that sound alike, but have different meanings.

a **piece** of pie

peace and quiet

Near-homophones are words that sound similar and are often confused when spelt, e.g. **affect** and **effect**.

Practice activities

1. Match up the pairs of homophones and near-homophones. The first one has been done for you.

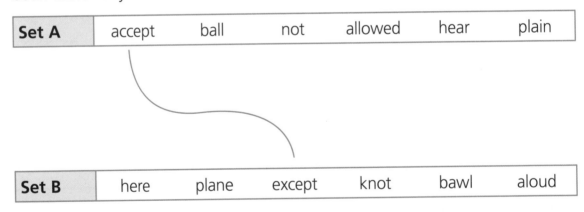

Set A	accept	ball	not	allowed	hear	plain

Set B	here	plane	except	knot	bawl	aloud

2. Underline the correct words in bold to complete each sentence. The first one has been done for you.

   a) The pirate **nose/knows** where the treasure is.

   b) The cut in her leg was starting to **heel/heal/he'll**.

   c) At the **fair/fare** they went on lots of rides.

   d) The boy had a **grate/great** new bike.

   e) He would not **accept/except** that the game was lost.

   f) You must not **medal/meddle** with the switches.

3. Write sentences using the given homophones.

Use a dictionary to help you to understand the meaning of each word.

a) peace _____

b) piece _____

c) brake _____

d) break _____

e) main _____

f) mane _____

g) groan _____

h) grown _____

i) heel _____

j) heal _____

k) here _____

l) hear _____

m) missed _____

n) mist _____

Test your spelling

Look at the words.

Say them aloud.

Cover the words.

Write them from memory.

Check your spelling.

accept	except	break
brake	peace	piece
affect	effect	
plain	plane	

More tricky words

Key to spelling

When it comes to spelling tricky words, you have to just learn them. Of course, you can help yourself to learn them by doing these things:

Listen for key sounds.

You will be able to hear some sounds to help you, e.g. a-c-d-n-t for the word **accident**.

Use a dictionary.

Finding the word will help you understand how it is spelt.

Think of similar words.

cycle – bi**cycle**

Spelling patterns may be the same.

Practice activities

1. Look at each word and write two closely related words. The first one has been done for you.

    a) conscience   _conscious_   _unconscious_

    b) certain   _____   _____

    c) surround   _____   _____

    d) discover   _____   _____

    e) describe   _____   _____

    f) behave   _____   _____

    g) inform   _____   _____

    h) care   _____   _____

    i) friend   _____   _____

More tricky words

2. Write a sentence containing each tricky word given.

a) calendar

_____

b) through

_____

c) experiment

_____

d) remember

_____

e) sentence

_____

f) building

_____

g) dictionary

_____

h) decorate

_____

Test your spelling

Look at the words.

Say them aloud.

Cover the words.

Write them from memory.

Check your spelling.

advertise	regular	knowledge
position	quantity	thought
weary	occasion	
medicine	extreme	

Mnemonics

Key to spelling

Mnemonics can help you to remember how to spell some tricky words.

big **e**lephants **c**an **a**lways **u**nderstand **s**mall **e**lephants

because

You can always adapt a mnemonic to make it more memorable for you.

If you have an image to go with a mnemonic, it helps you to remember it more easily.

Practice activities

1. Write the word each mnemonic helps you to spell.

a) **r**hythm **h**as **y**our **t**wo **h**ips **m**oving

_____

b) it **is land** surrounded by water

_____

c) **p**eople **e**at **o**range **p**eas **l**iterally **e**verywhere

_____

2. Create your own mnemonics for the given words. Draw an image to go with the mnemonic you create.

a) said

_____

_____

b) heart

_____

_____

c) earth

_____

_____

d) injure

_____

_____

Test your spelling

Look at the words.

Say them aloud.

Cover the words.

Write them from memory.

Check your spelling.

rhythm	island	earth
injure	heart	said
people	often	
sew	early	

More words to practise

This is an additional list of words, not covered in the *Test your spelling* sections, which you should also practise and learn to spell in Years 3 and 4. Like you did in the *Test your spelling* sections, practise them by **looking** at the words, **saying** them aloud, **covering** the words, **writing** them from memory and **checking** your spelling.

accident(ally)	address	answer	arrive
believe	breath	breathe	build
calendar	caught	centre	century
circle	describe	different	difficult
exercise	experience	favourite	forward(s)
grammar	guard	heard	height
history	imagine	important	increase
interest	learn	length	library
minute	natural	naughty	opposite
ordinary	particular	popular	pressure
probably	promise	quarter	question
recent	reign	remember	sentence
separate	special	straight	strange
strength	surprise	through	weight

Test practice

The tests here will help you to see how well you know your spelling. They provide practice for the spelling task at the end of Key Stage 2. (N.B. The spelling task in the KS2 SATs will have 20 words to find).
- Each sentence has a word missing.
- Ask somebody to read each missing word and sentence to you (these can be found in the answer booklet).
- Write the missing word in the space provided, making sure you spell it correctly.

Test 1

1. I can _____ very high.

2. The car needed a _____ this morning.

3. There is a nest in the _____.

4. The _____ platform was very busy.

5. The storyteller told us the _____ of the dragon.

6. It was _____ to snow outside.

7. Do not _____ during assembly.

8. The footballer fell _____.

9. _____ is everywhere around us.

10. There are _____ people at the swimming gala.

Test 2

1. Be careful not to trip over the _____.

2. Soon they would arrive at _____ destination.

3. A moat surrounded the _____.

4. It was _____ trying to fly the kite.

5. Many _____ people like using computers.

6. It is _____ to throw stones.

7. They made a meal for their elderly _____.

8. The _____ promised he would help people.

9. She could not _____ the gift.

10. I tried to _____ the wizard's name.

Test practice

Test 3

1. The _____ rescued the maiden from the monster.

2. Please close the _____ behind you.

3. They walked across the _____.

4. I have _____ my PE kit.

5. They lived _____ in the enchanted forest.

6. Her favourite team was top of the _____.

7. A pack of _____ surrounded the man.

8. Everybody moved to the _____ of the music.

9. The family looked through the holiday _____.

10. The sunglasses were a _____.

Test 4

1. Everybody _____ the bride looked pretty.

2. He was _____ sorry for the mess he had made.

3. They recognised the lady as a _____ actress.

4. It was a _____ wet day.

5. They were just _____ miles from home.

6. It was a lovely _____ day.

7. I will go _____ I want to.

8. We often have _____ at school.

9. Much _____ was caused by the loud bang.

10. The cruise ship was _____.

The practice activities in this book will have helped you to learn many words. There will, of course, be some spellings which you will still find difficult, so it is important to keep practising. Revisit the *Test your spelling* sections that appear throughout the book to help build your confidence.